HANDS-ON PROJECTS

FOR WILDLIFE WATCHERS

by Tamara JM Peterson
and Ruthie Van Oosbree

CAPSTONE PRESS
a capstone imprint

Dabble Lab is published by Capstone Press, an imprint of Capstone.
1710 Roe Crest Drive, North Mankato, Minnesota 56003
capstonepub.com

Library of Congress Cataloging-in-Publication Data
Names: Peterson, Tamara JM, author. | Van Oosbree, Ruthie, author.
Title: Hands-on projects for wildlife watchers / by Tamara JM Peterson and Ruthie Van Oosbree.
Description: North Mankato, Minnesota : Capstone Press, [2023] | Series: Adventurous crafts for kids | Includes bibliographical references. | Audience: Ages 8-11 | Audience: Grades 4-6 | Summary: "Calling all wildlife watchers! These hands-on projects will help you observe animals like never before. Make animal print casts to preserve outdoor animal tracks. Build a bug hotel to keep and observe insects before releasing them. Craft goggles to peek underwater. Use your creations on your next outdoor adventure!"— Provided by publisher.
Identifiers: LCCN 2022029002 (print) | LCCN 2022029003 (ebook) | ISBN 9781669004318 (hardcover) | ISBN 9781669004271 (pdf) | ISBN 9781669004295 (kindle edition)
Subjects: LCSH: Wildlife watching—Juvenile literature. | Natural history projects—Juvenile literature.
Classification: LCC QL60 .P48 2023 (print) | LCC QL60 (ebook) | DDC 590.72/34—dc23/eng/20220713
LC record available at https://lccn.loc.gov/2022029002
LC ebook record available at https://lccn.loc.gov/2022029003

Photo Credits
iStockphoto: Tim Speer, 28 (nature scene); Mighty Media, Inc.: project photos; Shutterstock: Jillian Cain Photography (blue jay), Front Cover, 8, Krumpelman Photography, Front Cover (wren), marutkin-v, 18 (fish)

Design Elements
Shutterstock: jekson_js, SHEKANDAR, VolodymyrSanych

Editorial Credits
Editor: Jessica Rusick
Designers: Emily O'Malley and Tamara JM Peterson

All internet sites appearing in back matter were available and accurate when this book was sent to press.

Printed and bound in the USA. PO5195

TABLE OF CONTENTS

GET READY FOR AN ADVENTURE!

Wildlife watching is always an adventure. Anything can happen out in the wilderness! Connecting with critters requires lots of supplies—including ones you can make yourself. So start planning your next wildlife adventure. You'll be sure to come prepared!

GENERAL SUPPLIES AND TOOLS

- beads
- bowls
- duct tape
- epoxy
- hot glue gun
- measuring cups and spoons
- scissors
- sticks
- string
- twine
- wire
- wood

CRAFTING TIPS

Follow these tips to make sure your projects are a success!

- Read all steps and gather all supplies before starting a project.

- Make sure you have permission to collect supplies such as sticks, rocks, and flowers from outside. Only use sticks that have been pruned or have fallen off a tree.

- Ask an adult to help when using hot or sharp tools.

ADVENTURE SAFELY

Wildlife watching is tons of fun! But before you embark on your adventure, make sure you know how to stay safe.

+ Never approach or follow animals. Research how to stay safe around animals you may encounter.

+ Don't feed animals unless you have permission to do so. Only feed animals with feeders and food that are safe for the animal.

+ When your wildlife adventures are away from your backyard, bring proper clothing, a compass and map, food and water, sunscreen, and a first aid kit.

+ Explore and rest in appropriate areas. Avoid damaging plant life on walks, learn to recognize dangerous plants, and follow trails when possible.

+ Stay with an adult at all times, and only go into water when an adult can supervise. If you get lost, stay put so others can find you.

+ Never drink water from lakes or streams without boiling or filtering it first. Don't drink stagnant water.

xBIRD FEEDER

Feeding birds can help them survive harsh winters, lower their stress levels, and give them energy for long migration flights. It also gives people an easy way to attract beautiful birds to their yards! Feed the birds in your area with this simple bird feeder.

MATERIALS ////////

- plastic planter with removeable base and drainage holes
- ruler
- craft knife
- plastic bottle with cap
- hot glue gun
- hole punch
- 24 inches (61 centimeters) thick wire
- birdseed

STEPS ////////

1 Remove the planter's base and set it aside until step 5.

2 Use the craft knife to cut the planter to 1 inch (2.5 cm) in height.

3 Cut four small holes near the bottom of the plastic bottle. The holes should be large enough for birdseed to fit through.

4 Hot glue the base of the plastic bottle to the inside of the planter.

5 Hot glue the cap of the plastic bottle to the inside of the planter's base.

6 To add a handle, punch two holes on opposite sides of the planter base's rim. Insert each end of the wire ½ inch (1.3 cm) into each hole. Bend the inserted wire sections into hooks.

7 Fill the bottle with birdseed. Put the cap and cover on the bottle and hang your feeder outside!

2

3

× TIP ×
Prevent bird diseases from spreading by keeping your feeder clean.

6

✱ UPCYCLED
BIRDBATH

All birds need water to drink. Birds also like to splash in water to clean their feathers. Visit your local thrift store to find colorful old dishware. Then make a beautiful, unique birdbath for your yard!

MATERIALS /////////

+ epoxy
+ parchment paper or paper plate
+ mixing stick
+ old, large serving bowl
+ small jar
+ glass pebbles (optional)
+ old vase
+ wooden dowel, 1–2 inches (2.5–5 cm) thick
+ water

STEPS /////////////

1 Mix the two parts of epoxy together on parchment paper or a paper plate.

2 Use the epoxy to glue the bottom of the serving bowl to the top of the jar. If you'd like, fill the jar with glass pebbles before gluing it.

3 Glue the bottom of the vase to the bottom of the jar.

4 Set the birdbath aside. Let the epoxy dry overnight.

5 Push the wooden dowel into the ground. Spread epoxy on top of the dowel. Place the vase upside down on the dowel.

6 Fill the serving bowl with water and wait for birds to come!

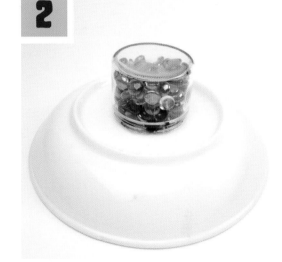

TIP

Birds need clean, fresh water to drink and for bathing. Be sure to clean the bowl of your birdbath regularly!

✖ BIRD
LOG CABIN

Habitat loss has left many birds without a place to nest. Give birds in your area a happy home with this rustic log cabin birdhouse. Attach your birdhouse to a post or hang it from a sturdy tree branch. Then wait for birds to visit!

MATERIALS ///////

- flat, square piece of scrap wood or particle board
- 4 rectangular pieces of wood, 8 inches (20 cm) long
- hammer and 4 nails
- twigs and sticks in various colors
- pruning shears
- hot glue gun
- small, flat stones (optional)
- scrap wood planks

STEPS ///////

1 Have an adult help you nail one rectangular piece of wood to each corner of the square scrap wood. This is the birdhouse's frame.

2 Use pruning shears to cut twigs and sticks that cover the sides of the birdhouse.

3 Hot glue the twigs and sticks to the frame to form four walls. Leave a 1½-inch (3.8-cm) square opening on one wall for the door.

4 If you'd like, glue small, flat stones to the sides of the scrap wood. Frame the door with four twigs.

5 Set out two wood planks so they are the width of your birdhouse. Glue additional wood planks across them to form a roof. Glue this to the top of your birdhouse. Your log cabin is ready for visitors!

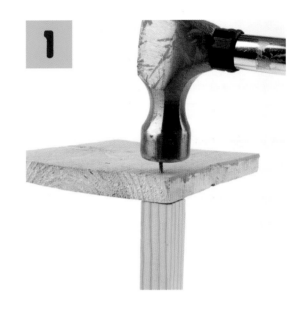

× TIP ×
If you want to attract a specific type of bird, research their preferences for door size, house height, and location of the house.

*BUG HOTEL

Birds aren't the only critters you can build a home for! Some helpful bugs pollinate plants and control pests. These bugs need safe spaces to live and lay eggs. Attract helpful bugs and give them shelter with a natural bug hotel!

MATERIALS ///////

- wooden box (lid is optional)
- paint and paintbrush
- white glue or wood glue
- natural materials such as sticks, pine cones, moss, and corn husks
- twine
- ruler
- scissors
- hot glue gun

STEPS ///////////

1 Paint the outside of the box so it will blend in with its surroundings. Don't paint the inside.

2 Pour glue to coat the bottom of the box. The glue should be about $1/8$ inch (0.3 cm) deep.

3 Carefully set your natural materials into the glue. Let the glue dry overnight.

4 Double knot the ends of a 2-foot (0.6-meter) piece of twine together. This is the hotel's hanger. Wrap a 1-foot (0.3-m) piece of twine around your hand several times. Remove it and tie a small piece of twine around the looped twine. Cut the loops open to make a tassel. Tie the tassel to the hanger and fit the hanger around the box.

5 Hot glue the twine onto the sides and bottom of your hotel.

6 Hang your bug hotel outside and see what kinds of bugs check in!

2

3

4

⁎ BEE
WATERING STATION

Carrying pollen from plant to plant can make a bee thirsty! But water is sometimes hard to find on hot summer days. Help bees get a refreshing drink with this watering station.

MATERIALS ///////

+ epoxy
+ mixing stick
+ parchment paper or paper plate
+ old plate
+ old vase with wide bottom
+ glass beads or stones
+ water

STEPS ///////////

1 Mix both parts of the epoxy together on parchment paper or a paper plate.

2 Glue the bottom of the plate to the bottom of the vase using the epoxy. Let the epoxy dry overnight.

3 Place glass beads or stones onto the plate. Bees can't swim, so this gives them a safe place to stand while they drink.

4 Set your bee watering station outside and fill it with water. Watch the bees fly in!

× **TIP** ×
Replace the water in your bee station every few days so it stays clean!

ANIMAL TRACK
✱ CASTING KIT

Next time you're in the woods, keep an eye on the ground. You might spot tracks from critters that roam the forest! With this casting kit, you can preserve the shape of an animal's prints. Save your animal tracks to remember your wildlife adventure!

MATERIALS ///////

+ plastic baggies
+ permanent markers
+ plaster of Paris
+ measuring cups
+ water
+ small bottles for liquid
+ medium plastic container with lid
+ duct tape

STEPS ////////////

1 Write "Plaster: Add ¼ cup water" on the plastic baggies. Put 1 cup (237 milliliters) of plaster of Paris into each bag. Seal the bags.

2 Put ¼ cup (59 mL) of water into each small bottle. Decorate the bottles and plastic container with duct tape and markers. Place your bags of plaster and bottles of water into your plastic container. This is your casting kit.

3 Bring the kit on your next hike. When you see an animal print you like, pour the water from one bottle into one baggie. Seal the bag and squish to mix.

4 Carefully pour the plaster mixture into the animal print. Put the plastic baggie and bottle back in the kit.

5 Let the plaster sit until it is solid enough to pick up, about one to two hours. Carefully place the print into your kit to carry home!

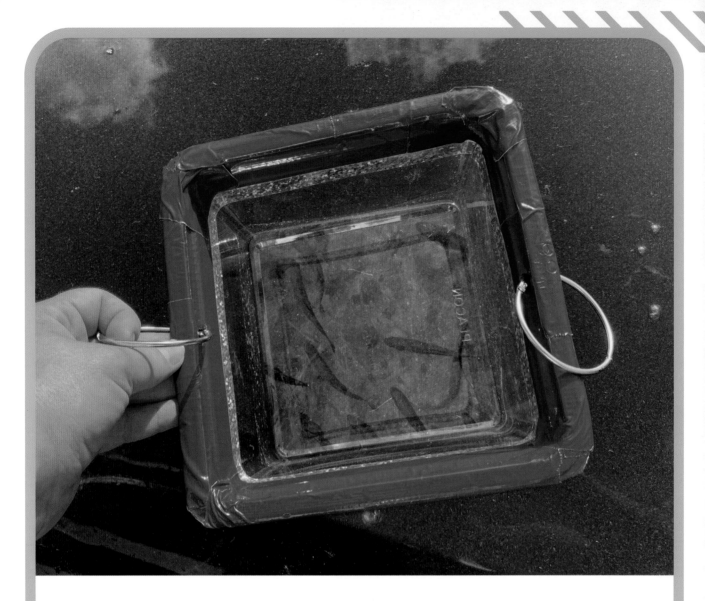

UNDERWATER
✳ VIEWER

It's often hard to see underwater creatures because of glare from the sun. With this handy underwater viewer, you can spot fish and other animals under the water's surface!

MATERIALS ///////

+ large, clear plastic container with lid removed
+ duct tape
+ decorative tape (optional)
+ scissors
+ hole punch or hammer and nail
+ 2 large binder rings

STEPS ///////////

1 Line the rim of the container with duct tape to strengthen it. With most containers, it is best to cut the tape into small pieces rather than trying to wrap one long piece around.

2 Decorate the sides of the container if you wish. Make sure not to cover the bottom of the container.

3 Using a hole punch or hammer and nail, punch holes in two opposite sides along the rim of the container.

4 Insert a binder ring into each hole. The rings serve as handles.

5 On your next wildlife adventure, submerge the container a few inches underwater. Look through the bottom for a view of underwater wildlife!

1

3

4

19

SPECIMEN
✗ INSPECTION KIT

Some animals are too small to see without a little help. Magnifying the details of bugs and other tiny critters can teach you a lot about the wildlife around you. Craft a kit to help you examine these creatures!

MATERIALS ////////

+ black and white paper
+ stapler
+ magnifying glass
+ tweezers
+ plastic pipettes
+ large plastic container
+ duct tape
+ permanent marker
+ clear plastic jars or petri dishes
+ pen

STEPS ////////////

1 Fold a sheet of black paper and a few sheets of white paper in half. Staple them together to make a small journal.

2 Decorate the journal, magnifying glass, tweezers, plastic pipettes, and container with duct tape and permanent marker.

3 Pack everything in the container along with the jars or petri dishes.

4 When you reach a stream, pond, lake, or puddle, use a pipette to transfer some water into a jar. When you find an interesting bug, gently pick it up with tweezers and place it into a jar.

5 Study each specimen with your magnifying glass. Record the specimen's location and your observations in the journal. When you're done, remember to put all specimens back where you found them!

*STICK
ANIMAL

Show your appreciation for wildlife by building your own miniature critter! Study your favorite animal closely. Then, use natural materials to bring your critter to life!

MATERIALS ///////

+ paper and pencil
+ sticks
+ pruning shears
+ hot glue gun
+ natural materials, such as dried flowers, leaves, moss, feathers, pine cones, stones, and twine

STEPS ////////////

1 Sketch an idea for your stick animal using paper and a pencil.

2 Cut sticks and hot glue them together to make the base structure for your animal. Make sure it is balanced and sturdy if you want to display your animal standing up.

3 Hot glue natural materials onto the stick structure to add details to the animal. Get creative! Think about the parts of your animal that are prickly, fuzzy, or other textures. Which natural materials could you use to create these textures?

4 Display your animal when it's finished!

× TIP ×
You do not have to make a real-life animal. You can also create one from your imagination!

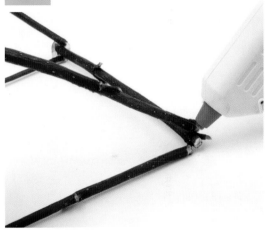

23

✖ GARDEN
DRAGONFLIES

It's fun to watch colorful dragonflies flutter around a garden. Ensure there are always dragonflies in sight with this wire and bead craft!

MATERIALS ///////

+ thick wire
+ ruler
+ wire cutter
+ needle-nose pliers
+ beads
+ metal stake

STEPS ///////////

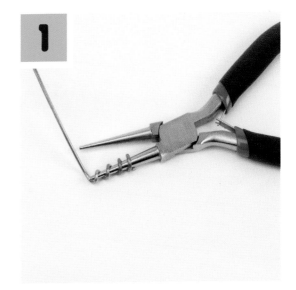

1 Cut 12 inches (30.5 cm) of thick wire using the wire cutter. Twist about 2 inches (5 cm) of one end of the wire around the pliers to make a spring shape. This will help attach your finished dragonfly to a metal stake.

2 String a bead onto the other end of the wire, stopping about 1 inch (2.5 cm) from the spring. This is the dragonfly's head. Bend the wire at the dragonfly's nose and twist the wire around the dragonfly's neck. Bend the spring down so it is perpendicular to the rest of the wire.

3 Add more beads to form the dragonfly's body. Twist a decorative spring into the remaining wire.

4 Cut another 12 inches (30.5 cm) of wire. Bend it into a symmetrical wing shape, adding twists and beads if you'd like.

5 Twist the wing wire onto the dragonfly's body behind the head. Attach the spring to the stake to display your dragonfly!

× HIDEAWAY
SHELTER

If you sit quietly and blend in with your surroundings, animals may not notice you. Construct a woodsy hiding place so you can observe animals without disrupting them!

MATERIALS ////////

- + trees
- + fallen limbs, branches, and long sticks
- + bark, moss, or pine needles

STEPS ///////////

1 Find a spot between two trees that stand a few feet away from each other.

2 Find a large limb on the ground that has a fork in one end. Lean the limb against one of the trees, using the forked end to secure it to the tree.

3 Repeat step 2 with a nearby tree. Have the two forked limbs meet each other between the two trees to create the structure of your shelter.

4 Lay branches across the top of your structure. Lean more branches up along one side to make a wall.

5 Place tree bark, moss, or pine needles on top of the structure to create a roof. Now you're ready to watch for wildlife!

× TIP ×

Never cut a living tree unless you are in a real survival situation. Stay safely away from wild animals.

*POLLINATOR FLOWER
SEED BOMBS

Pollinators are bugs and other animals that carry pollen from plant to plant. This helps plants produce seeds and fruit. Native flowers are important food sources for pollinators. With these seed bombs, you can plant native wildflowers to help the pollinators in your neighborhood!

MATERIALS

+ measuring cups and spoons
+ 1–2 tablespoons (15–30 mL) of wildflower seeds native to your area (these may include coneflower, dahlia, goldenrod, marigold, snapdragon, and sunflower)
+ 1 cup (237 mL) compost
+ 1 cup (237 mL) natural clay
+ small bowl
+ water

STEPS

1 Mix the seeds and compost together in a small bowl.

2 Take about ¼ cup (59 mL) of clay and make a disk. Pinch the sides up to form a small bowl.

3 Place 1 tablespoon (15 mL) of the seed mixture into the clay bowl.

4 Close the bowl into a ball by pushing the sides together.

5 Repeat steps 2 to 4 to make more seed bombs. Plant your seed bombs halfway into the ground in sunny locations.

6 Water the seed bombs every day until the plants are 6 inches (15 cm) tall. After that, water every few days. Stop watering when the plants are fully grown. Then watch for pollinators!

2

3

4

× **TIP** ×
Only plant seeds where you have permission to do so. Do not plant on public land.

✖ BIRD SUET CAKE

Suet cakes are mixtures of different foods in a hardened block. They help supplement birds' diets in colder months when their typical foods are harder to find. Make your own suet cakes to help birds survive the winter!

INGREDIENTS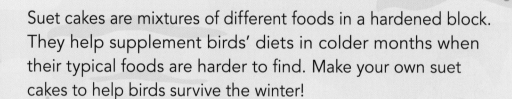

+ 1 cup (237 mL) shortening
+ 1 cup (237 mL) peanut or almond butter
+ 1 cup (120 grams) flour
+ 2 cups (473 mL) birdseed
+ 1 cup (237 mL) oatmeal or cornmeal

MATERIALS

+ measuring cups
+ large mixing bowl
+ mixing spoon
+ 4 small bowls
+ freezer
+ mesh produce bag
+ string and large sewing needle
+ ruler
+ scissors

STEPS

1 Mix the ingredients together in a large bowl.

2 Put 1½ cups (355 mL) of the mixture into each small bowl. Press the mixture down.

3 Leave the bowls in the freezer overnight.

4 Use the sewing needle to thread 12 inches (30 cm) of string around the top of the mesh produce bag. This will make a drawstring bag that can be reused for all of the suet cakes.

5 Take one bowl out of the freezer and remove the suet cake. Put the cake into the drawstring bag and pull the top closed. Hang the bag from a tree in winter for birds to enjoy! Replace the suet cake when needed.

× TIP ×
These suet cakes are best for freezing winter days, as they will melt at warm temperatures.

READ MORE

Carson, Mary Kay. *Wildlife Ranger Action Guide: Track, Spot & Provide Healthy Habitat for Creatures Close to Home.* North Adams, MA: Storey Publishing, 2020.

Rivers, Kristine. *Exploring Birds Activity Book for Kids: 50 Creative Projects to Inspire Curiosity & Discovery.* Emeryville, CA: Rockridge Press, 2021.

Tordjman, Nathalie. *The Book of Tiny Creatures.* New York: Princeton Architectural Press, 2021.

INTERNET SITES

Animals: kids.nationalgeographic.com/animals

Engaging Wildlife and Animal Activities for Children: mothernatured.com/children

San Diego Zoo Wildlife Explorers: sdzwildlifeexplorers.org

ABOUT THE AUTHORS

RUTHIE VAN OOSBREE

Ruthie is a writer and editor who loves nature and animals. She has rescued baby squirrels, a baby bunny, and a big brown bat. In her free time, she enjoys exploring city parks, reading, and playing the piano.

Ruthie lives with her husband and three cats in Minnesota.

TAMARA JM PETERSON

Tami grew up traveling, camping, fishing, and hiking, and still does so whenever possible. She has been to 46 of the 50 states, including three weeklong trips into the Boundary Waters Canoe Area in Minnesota.

Tami lives with her husband, two daughters, and a cat named Cliff.